THEY SING TO HER BONES

The New Issues Press Poetry Series

Editor	Herbert Scott
Associate Editor	David Dodd Lee
Advisory Editors	Nancy Eimers, Mark Halliday William Olsen, J. Allyn Rosser
Assistant to the Editor	Rebecca Beech
Assistant Editors	Allegra Blake, Matthew Hollrah, Alexander Long, Amy McInnis, Tony Spicer, Tom West
Editorial Assistants	Laura Maloney, Lydia Melvin, Bonnie Wozniak
Business Manager	Michele McLaughlin
Fiscal Officer	Marilyn Rowe

The New Issues Press Poetry Series is sponsored by The College
of Arts and Sciences, Western Michigan University, Kalamazoo, Michigan

First Edition, 2000.

ISBN: 0-932826-87-3 (paperbound)

Library of Congress Cataloging-in-Publication Data:
Manesiotis, Joy
They Sing to Her Bones/ Joy Manesiotis
Library of Congress Catalog Card Number (99-076766)

Art Direction and Design:	Tricia Hennessy
Production:	Paul Sizer The Design Center, Department of Art College of Fine Arts Western Michigan University
Printing:	Courier Corporation

THEY SING TO HER BONES

JOY MANESIOTIS

New Issues Press

WESTERN MICHIGAN UNIVERSITY

for my parents

and in memory:
Eleni Peros Manesiotis
Iro Plyttas Caloyer

Contents

III

Foreword

First, a few thoughts about what Joy Manesiotis' poems are not. They're neither speedy nor tongue-in-cheek. They take no truck with the famous rush—that vivid panic—of American life that has drawn many good poets to the fragment, the non-sequitur, the ironic aside, the sensational detail. These poems aren't *out there*; they don't chat. They refuse, in their stubborn way, to narrow to the self and whatever agonies lie trapped there. They're not about personality; we're not hypnotized by a voice exactly, though belief is another matter. And popular culture? Not one reference to McDonald's lives here, nothing of television or Starbuck's. No one's at the movies or wishing to be. No traffic jams, no caller ID.

In short, Manesiotis' poems, at first glance, don't feel particularly *au courant*, post-modern, post-contemporary, post-post whatever we'd claim— if we were in a naming mood—for our small breath of years as one century turns into another, as we look backward or forward in our squared-off Janus moment, getting hopelessly confused, or dreamy, or sad. Yet. Yet for all the ways Manesiotis' poems are *not*, there looms up the rich, multiple ways they *are*. And how to begin describing that?

With history, perhaps, though not the *big box* of history but the smaller, messy, less elegant one crowded with family, with grandparents, aunts, uncles, endless cousins and odd old-world habits superimposed on the new. Manesiotis is only one generation removed from that most basic American fact that almost everyone in this country came from elsewhere; that we who follow are all mutts, genetically or culturally or both. She's in that familiar nevertheless curious position—grandchild of immigrants and exiles, in this case from Greece—and she uses it without sentimentality to get at the sweet and the dark of such an equation: what is left behind never quite translates.

This is an American book, about American experience. But several pieces do take us directly back. There are, for instance, the lovely monastery poems based on visits to those 16th century sites in the mountains of Thessaly in northern Greece, places—and poems—which aren't lovely at all, really, but savagely beautiful, one monastery's frescos showing saints "skinned or boiled alive set against/the deep blue that calms the heart," their relics "skulls under glass." And how, as an American, even a Greek-American, to take in these

3

images? To accept the blessing of the one-eyed monk there? Such questions and connections get stranger and closer to heart in the remarkable "Return to *Loganíko*," a long poem whose sections layer the life of Eleni Peros Manesiotis, the poet's grandmother, against Manesiotis' own pilgrimage to the family's village. The amazing beginning of this piece underscores the governing tone of the whole collection—its wonder, its deep elegiac pull, its careful distance—as it records Eleni's apparent childhood death and her startling recovery at the funeral itself where the girl "flutters and rolls/her head back and forth" under the priest's touch, the "*stavrós*, holy oil," the women calling to her, the child calling out "to the one/to call out to: *mother, mother*."

This calling out is something that recurs throughout the book in various ways, from the Greek Orthodox practice recorded in "Lament: *Moirología*" where it is the women again who are the source of song in sacred ritual ("they sing/to her hair turned white, to her hands broken in work./ They sing to her bones . . ."), to the more personal elegies, cast in direct address, that work with reserve and great delicacy to bring back both the life and death of friends. But it's more than invocation. In "On Your Birthday, Four Months After Your Death," the poet's final singing out—"I will place you there, Costa, where/I want to sleep, on the orchid´s plush cheek,/three petals curved. . . ." —is brilliantly balanced against an earlier emphatic listening by telephone to the friend in his coma, to his hard breathing ("as if you/knew anymore what a phone was"), and then, in memory, to the vital, fully alive Costa, who, on the line from New York, once coached the speaker in the traditional Greek dances as she prepared for her wedding—"step, cross back,/three steps, kick: the *kalamatianó*—memory in my feet, each of us/sliding across the floor, cradling the phone, you/saying, *yes, yes that's it.*" Perhaps it's not surprising after all that the English words "mourning" and "memory" share the same Greek root, *memera*, "to care." It's remembering such happiness—and the love which results—that counters grief.

But a comforting balance isn't always possible. Manesiotis' more hopeless vision is revealed in a piece like "Angels Who Lie Down Upon Us," another elegy that speaks eloquently, though here, it's not about the dead as much as the dying, capturing that moment when the body's terrible failure goes public and there's no way but silence—or secret outcry—to respond.

. . . you mean to say *yes, yes,*
but instead *no*, attenuated, deep
in your throat, wrenches out and I watch it
warp back through the tunnels of your brain,
and your face, how it twists,
soft clay someone has slid a thumb along,
smudged with effort, with shame.

And where are the angels who lie down among us?
Why are they not singing?

As much as song guides these poems—and often Manesiotis' early
training as a musician is obvious, especially in wonderfully fractured pieces
where a more lyric sound is keyed, as in "Fugue," "O Beautiful Boy" or in
"Fledgling"—a certain "not singing" is an equal force here, one that finds in
stillness and its children (painting, photographs, scenes meticulously sketched
from the past) a kind of eternal, seemingly wordless presence. Again, there's
another discipline possibly behind this, Manesiotis' work in art and design,
and later, in film editing. But it's also that elegaic edge coming back to power
the eye and throw the world in part shadow. Such pieces as "Worry Beads" and
"On the Beach" are filled with a child's energy for detail. Still, there's an adult
sadness in the elaboration, a sense that we can only freeze what is lost
forever—the large extended family pinned between cultures, its camaraderie,
food, its mysterious worry beads, and evil eyes pinned to undershirts, then
things that casually backdrop a room, those old headboards, for instance,
with a woman's profile in the center—images specific to one time and place. In
another piece, Manesiotis writes directly as a painter as she darkly deconstructs
Botticelli's use of light, her own training thrown in relief. "In art school, we
learned to see, to sense the eight colors/inside sienna or Payne's gray, to
hone the focus . . . ." And so, in another poem, the speaker observes in an
old photograph of her parents before her birth something hidden and
overwhelming in her mother's face, in "the tilt of her head." That the poem
begins by intuiting her father's technique—"He must have held the camera
out at arm's length . . . so fully do their faces/fill the frame and so soft the
light . . ."—suggests something of Manesiotis' own sense of boundary and its
rewards, a certain tact uncommon in poetry these days.

5

I say "uncommon" because such tact is a matter of careful, detailed observation in a world that would rather gulp the grand bits down. She takes her time and keeps things at that "arm's length." Call it reverence or wonder. Maybe her training as a painter has done this. Maybe her double vision as a child of two cultures—the discomfort of that, but its richness too—has given her an acute awareness of clear distances and sorrows and complexities in herself and in others. In the poem "Voodoo," the poet watches from a high window as a stranger, a young Haitian in some inexplicable ritual in the New York street chants and shouts—"Remember: it's November and cold/and . . . he doesn't care, head tranced back and body open/to rain." But then, he sees her watching, and the poet suddenly grasps what he must see *in* her, in this clash of passions and beliefs—"a semaphore/from the dead world: concrete and steel,/alien, ruthless, white." Sometimes, there is only the bare, fierce fact of a thing. Manesiotis lets that stand too.

Marianne Boruch

Acknowledgments

Grateful acknowledgment is made to the following journals in which these poems first appeared, some in slightly different versions:

The American Poetry Review: "Behind Anger"

The Antioch Review: "Voodoo"

The Colorado Review: "Loosestrife"

Denver Quarterly: "Fugue"

The Journal: "Anesthesia"

Marlboro Review: "Fledgling," "Lament: *Moirología*"

The Threepenny Review: "On Your Birthday, Four Months After Your Death"

The Virginia Quarterly Review: "Not Yet Dead"

I would like to thank The Ragdale Foundation for residencies, and the New York Foundation for the Arts, the University of Redlands, and The Graves Awards for fellowships that helped me complete this book.

And special thanks to Marianne Boruch, Brigit Pegeen Kelly, Ellen Bryant Voigt, Renate Wood, Andrew Ramer and Jan Kristiansson for their generous encouragement and suggestions. And to Beach, abiding gratitude.

9

One

The Road

Past the house and further, the white road,
not the cobbled lane, curving tight

between blinding white walls on the island.
Rough tan block, the house yellowish

against the blue sky, a wood porch, capped
by brick tiles, the porch leaning against the road,

the grape arbor before it, tangled and sweet.
This is where the sadness lies, on this

road, in its jagged curve, in the pattern
woven by the vines and cast onto the smooth white,

crushed stones, ground to a fine dust, a powder
finer than the mist that rises

up the mountain in the mornings,
through the fig orchards, ghosting the olive trees.

On the Beach

Iphegenia came every few days to join
the group sprawled under the umbrellas: blond bangs
sprouting from a *babushka*, and stiletto heels,
she sat down to the card game, dealing
onto the lid of the cooler, blue shadow
and black liner making a dash off her eye. My brother,
in the ocean on a raft, was always the farthest one out;
an adult would run down to the chair on stilts and signal
the lifeguard: whistle, motion him back. Under the umbrellas:
blankets, cold *keftedes* sandwiches, coffee, lemonade,
parents, aunts, uncles, grandmother, rafts and inner tubes,
and four girls—cousins and sisters—wandering in and out, one asleep
in the shade, another digging in the sand,
my bachelor uncle pushing me through the surf in an inner tube.
When the wave hit, I was looking back
toward shore, waving to my father
in his yellow trunks; then I had slipped through, balled up:
first my head hit the ocean floor, then an elbow,
a knee, the water solid from churned sand, scraping
my back, spun up and over again, squeals and laughter
through the pound and roar, then shouts,
while hands reached, tugged me out, until I coughed,
spit water, let out a cry.

When the air turned soft, we'd drag everything
the block and a half home, line up
by the outdoor shower, going in twos. After, we'd lie down
in the blue room on beds with blue headboards, a woman's profile
in black at the center, and watch our mothers dress:
they brushed out auburn hair, lined their lips red,
pulled on girdles and slips, while we asked questions,
picked dresses for them to wear, or,
curled against each other, our mothers' voices

washing over us, a viscous liquid to float in,
we turned through our dreams,
and swam into sleep.

Coma

We say *slipped into a coma*, as if
it were a long slide he slipped down, a chute
curved and snaking, carrying him into twilight, into
a darkness we can't reach. Walled off, even before this slide,
moving among us mute, hardly moving, hardly able to move,
his body splaying in four directions instead of one, instead
of *forward, to walk, walking.* Here he is breathing and here
we guess what to say, how to act, what he wants: maybe it isn't
darkness but light, green and blue, the body
easier to bear, the freight of matter lifting away.
Betrayal. The body's will moving it, halfway
to the other side and we are pulling,
pulling to hold him here. There is this tunnel, this chute,
the pain born from trying to span it, the gulf
widening between us and him
breathing for us, who hover around the body, reassuring,
but what do we know? what do we know of where he is,
of where he is going? what he needs
is for us to open the hand—

Costa, Costa—it's your name calling.

Roussanou

In Orthodoxy, the spirit is born again and again
in light, the resurrection the moment
we gather around. *Roussanou* rises sheer
from the face of rock, the all-black
habits of the women swirl back across the two
thin footbridges that connect it to the world. Hand hewn
stone, rougher than its smooth rock pedestal, a thousand
feet up, the natural rock gives way to the monastery's
wall as one continuous movement toward God.
No way to reach here. The edge of the monastery
is the edge of this world.
                                    Slow turn through the seasons,
the offices turn through the days and nights,
the Liturgy ascends the hours of winter, predawn,
and opens the radiant windows of spring: matins,
vespers, *esperinós*: deep ocean, swelling through the moon's
rotation, the sun's blinking eye, coasting the women's voices.
The earth's song breathes through the stone, the small
light at dusk illuminates each square window
cut in stone. Hands murmur
over each lantern, and light spills
from the windows, over the walls, down
the face of rock, into the valley: pine trees, silence,
the village *Kastráki* kneeling in its shade.

                                    Shade. Underside of light.
Light's twin, the other child of God. The iron door locks
shut, the women pass through blank corridors.
Y Panayía: The Virgin Mother, head sideways, three
fingers raised, gazes from the icon, blessing the cell:
bed, chair. A square of night sky floats in the wall. It is here
the woman is caught: the endless movement out,
the song inside: she looks out but sings

inward, sings inward: *proséfkome*:
a whole universe to weave through: planets, stars:
endless distance inside.

Return to *Loganíko*

The terrace was blue
on the house in *Loganíko*. The terrace
propped against the whitewashed wall, floated
above the second story, small heaven facing
the inner courtyard.
                                    Eleni played there,
leaned there, paying out the string
of the kite. Bright diamond rising and dipping
against the blue plate of sky, body
stretching into air. She reaches, strokes
the air, falls. Eleni crumpled on the hard dirt
path: blue lips, pillow of blood. Her mother,
the one to call out to, bent over, the sign of the cross:
stavrós, two fingers and thumb pursed: forehead, waist,
shoulder, shoulder: *the last touch, the nailed hand.*

Eleni's mother and sisters bathe her, they dress her
in the Sunday dress, they lay her in the coffin
in the house, light candles around it, bring
the Virgin and the Child to sit
at the head. The lament rises up, the old women,
the young women, the widows crouch in black—ravens
swaying in the corner, they rock back and forth, their voices
climbing into the air, they sing
the song of the child, keening, opening
the door, finding passage to the other side.

The priest. The village. They bring fish, olives.
They bring wine, *krasí*. The wind rises
through the olive groves, the silver leaves waving and waving,
goodbye to the child, *goodbye, goodbye.*

The *psalti*'s voice lifts against the morning, scales
the steps of the women's voices. Eleni's mother
sits in the dark corner, her daughters flanked
around her while the altar boy swings the beaten gold
censor, frankincense puffing in small clouds
that blue the air. Bent over, about to mark
Eleni's forehead with oil, the priest:
about to touch lightly, *stavrós*, holy oil,
the cross on her brow.

But she flutters and she rolls
her head back and forth. *Eleni*. The women
have called her back, they opened the door
between the worlds with their voices, they held it
open for the child. *Eleni*.
Eleni. The child is back. She is coming back.
She watches blue wreathes float
in the air, her eyes swim around the room, she
calls out to the one
to call out to: *mother, mother*.

*

Such a strange well rising—all that was Greek
now touched and moving, and with it,

the long road, the emptiness of no place, no
home. But *Eleni, Eleni*. Parts of it

live in me: bottles of holy water
to bless each house, the blue eye, shield

against the evil one, shreds of language that rise
in my throat, the music from the villages, and

zembékiko, slow slide across the dirt floor, sway
and finger snap. *Taygetos. Loganíko*:

Balcony of the Mountain: *Georgitsi*. The house
perched against the side: tile roof, fire pit,

broken boards. *Georgaki. Eleni*. The children
who went down into the world, down from the mountain,

down from the spring, the mill, family, away
away. Into the other world.

Psalti's voice calling atonal, nasal,
pitch and fall, ascending step

by step. The altar is forbidden to the women,
whose voices rise instead in lament,

in childcall, in waves through the *horyó*,
and swallows swoop the fading light

of the sky. Now, this is not home, and
I am left the thin track to walk, path

and boundary, between *this* and *that*, this life
and that, mountain and sea, bird chirp and

cicada call, mingling in the hollow
space, the circle of my arms.

*

Here is a village, *horyó* , in August, on an island,
houses stacked on the hillside, blank windows, eyes

staring out, the quiet hours, deep blue shutters
drawn against the heat, and red tile roofs scattered
among the gray shale ones, boats plying in
and out of the harbor: *Icarus, Flying Dolphin*.
At night, *cosmos*, so many *cosmos*, tourists throng
the waterfront: *volte*, turn and walk, and later,
young prowlers on motorbikes, hair cut just so,
from Italy, England, fling their bodies
to American disco music in Club 52 and VIP's, bass
booming over the harbor: a Mediterranean vacation,
days and nights in a small hotel, whitewashed,
with wooden beds, a hot plate and a washstand,
and afternoons on a stretch of pebbled beach,
chestnut goats scaling the cliffside, fish
like silver dollars suspended in the transparent sea.

*

At thirteen, Eleni is carried,
carried in to see Georgaki, her knees
buckling. He is a man. She is to marry him. She remembers:
waking in a narrow wooden space, head pounding,
the scratch of her church dress, the keen
lacing the air, candlelight and incense, the priest's
face breathing over her.

She knows. She will never see *Loganíko* again.
Here, in Pittsburgh, everything is red brick, hard—
hard surfaces, hard shiny stoves, hard sounds
to form the language. Greek is a song
from the back of the throat, a deep well
running clear and cool against the hot dry air.
But English is all up front, against
the teeth and lips, even the long 'A'

a hard sound that asks for tightness
in her cheeks, the sky of her mouth open.

*

The wind shushes through the olive trees,
and the cicadas whir out their call, constant,
dithering, a dirge the heat calls from them.

They cannot stop. They must continue,
the whir and click of legs and wings,
over and over, crescendo and release

inside the larger sound, back and forth,
hundreds of tiny saws in the branches.

*

Georgaki's deep laugh fills the room. Eleni hears
the goats high up on the hillside, she hears
the fish slap water, the wind
shaking the olive branches. His Greek is from the mountain,
Taygetos, the vowels threshed in the huge grinding stones
of his family's mill. She is to marry him.
The consonants roll through like grain. She will
marry him. The syllables float up, buoyant
in the light on the mountain.   23

*

The Americans have bought a house, of course,
and with the German, say, *It's too early to eat in Greece*.
But they are *xéni*, foreigners, not the inside, not
the hours of work that turn the hands old,

that make the old woman walk on permanently bent knees.
They want to preserve 'the tradition,' they fly
back to their American house on a jumbo jet, they dye
their hair black, they try to speak the language.
The other vacationers just buzz over the island,
riding hills covered in plum trees, branches
weighted with richness, ochre turning to plum,
tart to sweet, and almonds, fuzzy green diamonds
casing the meat inside, not yet ripe, not yet
ready, like the green buds of olives clinging hard
to the branches of the trees, twisted and hollow.

*

Eleni stands in front of the gas stove, its enamel desert
stretching in front of her. She turns the knob, hears
the hiss, the small blue flames thud
around the circle. Eleni sees the fireplace
at home in *Loganíko*, the hardpacked floor, her mother
sitting on a stool by the fire pit,
stirring the *avgolémono* soup, the spoon
cutting a swath through egg and lemon, the bubbling
surface a yellow swirl like the mark on the blue
eye, the one Eleni wears to ward off the other,
the evil eye: covetous glance, the one thrown
in love and meant to harm.

*

At night, the music collides
as it drifts up from the harbor: *rembétika* here

and American disco music here, and electrified,
Greek pop music: it rolls together

in cacophony, floats on the wind currents
that carry goat bells and British voices and the whine

of *papakis*. In Glossa, far up the island, a night
of traditional dances: the schoolyard flooded with light,

a stage with a cafe-painted backdrop, the risers
packed with people, the children

running the flat cement interlude in packs.
On stage, two 'boys' from the village

linking arms, *hasápiko*, they leap in unison: *maleness*:
only the steps, not the ardor, as the others

simulate the *cafenío* behind them, and only one
young man keeps his place in the dance:

not like their grandfathers, now in the bleachers, who
this afternoon, like every afternoon, sat in the *cafenío*

arguing politics, hands cupped around glasses of *ouzo*, who
still could outdance these boys, who in their prime, hissed

and stamped, leapt and crouched, twirling, faces
split in smiles, heads thrown back.

*

Georgaki went back. For two years,
he went back. But Eleni said *no*, she
didn't go back, *no*, she said, *no*.

*

The door of the streetcar clanks open
in front of her: first pain shoots through
her belly. She commands her right leg
to lift, to step up, to move her *up*
and *in*, but no, no, it won't
move. The fist in Eleni's belly grabs
again, knife twist, deep heat. She is
on the street, a leg of lamb under one arm,
riding on her hip; her other arm cradles Elias,
firstborn, and her fingers clasp under the child
turning in utero, swimming down
toward the tunnel out. Elias will die young.
Eleni will mourn him every day of her life. Georgaki
will never dance again. But now, she stands frozen,
on the street, unable to step into the streetcar,
people jostling past her, traffic in the street, all strangers.

*

Terraces. Levels of terraced land, the pale wash
of dried oats, strips of grass, *prásina*,
half circles: gray stone walls shape each level, one stone
laid upon the next, cupping silver-gray olive trees, and above,
the backdrop of green: pine, oak, poplars
shaking their disk-like leaves, sycamores, figs,
each leaf an outstretched hand. Water, water:
narrow stone aqueduct overhead: rough hewn, hand-
made, to run it off, the underground bubbling
with water, a spring feeding this land, so high up,
Balcony of the Mountain, rising above the Laconian Plain
which stretches away: ochre, sienna, forest green, and the dark
spines of cypress thrusting up, clusters of punctuation.

*

Georgaki is in bed. He is old, old, one hundred
and four. And here, the doorbell ringing and ringing,
and Eleni greets the guests, while her children,
their wives and husbands, their children all
bustle around to fix the food, put one large candle
on the cake: Happy 70th Anniversary.
Lewis serves champagne to Georgaki, everyone holds
a glass, the priest performs the switching of the rings
again: his on her finger, hers on his finger, marrying them
once more, and then *S'ya mas* and *Xronia Pollá*,
the congratulations: *Many Years*,
the family gathered: fourteen aunts and uncles, fifteen
first cousins and more and more, they're laughing,
they're clapping, they're holding up their glasses.

*

It was raining. I made the journey
back but you were gone, Eleni, gone. I saw
your house, its blue terrace
above the white lane, high up in *Taygetos*.
Was your ten-year-old body imprinted on the air
held still behind the shutters?
It was raining. I stood in the mud outside
your house. Then I turned away.

Not Yet Dead

Christmas Eve I get the call from your family,
asking me to write a "bio"—for what? for the funeral
home, but you are not yet dead, barely skirting
the edge of a coma, circling the dark lake: are you
walking around it to keep from going in or
searching for the most hospitable water, the least
deep, the least cold? I begin *Charles Gus . . .*
but leave off the time and date of death, the first
piece of information, and stare at the computer screen's
glacial flicker as you stare at the ceiling, three thousand
miles away. I want to write: *Dear Costa,*
No, not my shoulders, but the front
of my shoulders, collarbone, that wing
across the front of my body aches for you.
It starts to flap as I write out what you've done,
danced and choreographed several projects
not yet dead, the air slamming against my chest,
the wing, slow and steady, beating the air to froth, wind
rushing by my ears, *handmade dolls toured Europe,*
the wing, those hollow bones unfurling, burgundy feathers
rowing down through wind as if it were water, the lake
whipped up, surface churning and burnished, metallic
green, gunmetal gray, *survived by Michael, Constantine,*
the clouds roiling over the lake, where on the far shore,
service, Greek Orthodox Church, dusk,
you stand dark and small, where, afraid, you begin to step in
and the wing extends, shadows the lake,
but cannot sweep you back.

Loosestrife

Loosestrife blankets the fields; its companion,
goldenrod, yellow and free. The loosestrife releasing

its purple shoots, its heather-like brush, its loose
strife, purple gone loose upon the world, strife

floating over each field as the hawk floats low
on the thermals. Inconsolable, loose grief, wild

and keening across the wind currents that brush
the earth, brush laden with this violet grief, falcon

hanging stilled on a rush of air, one current
countering it, impulse and counterimpulse, the pulling to

the pushing away: the first lesson of science:
positive ends nudge apart, opposites unite.

But the charged metal pulls the *other* closer, the *other*
pushes away, as if *this* were a law of nature,

as if it could be any other way.

Lament: *Moirología*

The women throw themselves back and forth,
their bodies saplings in wind, but they are
close to the grave and they sing to death: *Oh slowly,*
oh mournfully, I will begin lamenting
spirits rising to wail with them, the ghosts of their voices
loosed across dusty paths, paving stones traced in white.
shouting out your sorrows, Mother—one by one! rising
and rising, the pitch of voices a high wind
on the mountain, a breath winding the olive groves, the keen
pushing against the blue doors, against the cool mud wall
of the church, the women's voices as one, pushing
against the men's dark clothes, the priest's slow footstep:
the men shuffle in the corner, the women fall back
and forth, dragging nails across their cheeks, *Ah Mother!*
you knew how to embroider the sky with all its stars!
they sing to the one who has passed over, they sing
to her hair turned white, to her hands broken in work.
They sing to her bones. First they must bury her. Day after day
they will clean the grave. Month by month. Washing,
washing. *My mother has travelled*
far away. One day they will roll back the dirt. They push back
the dirt. They reach in, fingers against bone. And they lift
her bones, one by one, sweet digits of her fingers, bowl of her pelvis:
To whom can I call out? they wash her bones, they rinse
each one. Cradle her skull. Her skull
passed from hand to hand, soothed in each lap, rough
palms cupped over the crown. *Ah Mother!*

And who here will say
the women cannot sing to her now?

On Your Birthday, Four Months After Your Death

Yes, she held the phone to your ear and
we heard you breathing, hard
and quick, as if someone were pushing your chest,
as if a pump forced you to breathe. And we
talked, as if you could hear us, as if
you understood why our voices came
through the hard plastic instrument, as if you
knew anymore what a phone was. Years ago
I stood in my living room, listening
through the phone to Greek songs you played
and we danced—you in New York, me in Boston—you coaching
me through the traditional dances—step, cross back,
three steps, kick: the *kalamatianó*—memory in my feet, each of us
sliding across the floor, cradling the phone, you
saying, *yes, yes that's it*. This
before my wedding, where, when the *bouzouki* sounded,
high-pitched, nasal, you leaped and stamped, whirled
mid-air, led the circle of dancers—hiss and *oopah!*
That day I carried the phalaenopsis, the pure
white, the moth orchid, rush
of white water, filament of wings, and everything
seemed possible, the radiant
silk of that horizon, as if the arc
the orchid traced could map the world,
as if we knew at all what lay ahead. Now
I will place you there, Costa, where
I want to sleep, on the orchid's plush cheek,
three petals curved, phalaenopsis, most beautiful,
the orchid's white tongue, they say: the world
is calm and just, they say: there is no end to beauty,
they say: everything is possible,
oh sweet wild scarf of white, swirl of velvet water, let me
lay my friend there, yes, I will place you there, Costa,
curled and sleeping.

31

Two

Where I Want to Be

In the black-and-white postcard, the 1957 Lincoln Premiere
is stately, parked at the end of an asphalt lot
by the beach, Venice, California.
The angle shows the profile of the car—
sleek, black, and finned—
and its chrome bumpers nose the small graffiti
on the curbside stops.
Ocean fills the windows, bleaching
to a lighter gray,
and a few lumpy palm trees stand off to the left,
black as the car—six shorter ones scattered
and four tall ones in the middle,
all with hairy trunks and tops like giant shaggy orchids,
and the ocean stretches out behind them,
behind the Lincoln, the expanse of asphalt
in front, and a hint of sand between.
Sky fills two-thirds of the space, the clouds
broken by a patch of lighter sky—perhaps the sun
although it looks like a cloudy day,
the kind of day when a walk on the beach makes you
the most alone in the world, forsaken.
If you had children, you wouldn't bring them here
because you need to keep that wild loneliness
from entering their small bodies so soon,
keep the emptiness from opening in their chests,
keep them safe a little longer.

After Botticelli's *Madonna and Child with an Angel*

But it's the angel, coming in from the lower
left corner, his brown cap of curls framed by the edge
of the canvas, the first line of the composition. He is
looking up, hands clasped before him, his face
hopeful, mouth curved in a half smile. The only one
without a halo is the angel, the Madonna's and child's
two shimmering aureoles an echo of the angel's earthbound
umber hair. Upper left, the eye is pulled
by the dark contours of the Umbria, layered in ochre
and moss green, a small square receding as the hills
of Sienna roll away toward Florence. The Botticelli room
in the Uffizi Gallery is struck with light, canvas after canvas
radiating: propped on easels, scattered throughout the room, fixed
on the walls; in a hallway draped in tapestries, punctuated
with sculptures, the doorway a choir of light,
and amid all this chaos of art, the room lifts up, serene
in its radiance, the Venus coasting on her half-shell, the Madonnas'
eyes cast down. Botticelli must have touched something
to do with grace, must have seen the soul's lantern
sliding just beneath the flesh, and known it
to be other than Savonarola's flame, hungry to consume desire.
In art school, we learned to see, to sense the eight colors
inside sienna or Payne's gray, to hone the focus
until the hand became an extension of the eye, the brush
travelling along the model's forearm. We wanted to live
inside the luminous energy of light. But some are born
with it inside them, and offer it up, as it radiates now
off the porcelain skin of the Madonna and child, rendering
the Prussian blue—and a little ochre, a little white—of her sleeve,
the patch of carmine at her breast and cuff.

Anesthesia

I know nothing about this.
After we had fit the tiny headsets, like buttons
into my ears, and the Gregorian Chant poured out—
the young boys' voices like angels', unearthly,
the older ones earthbound, their voices tied
to dirt and grass, singing roots and trees
while the younger voices floated above, piercing
clouds and sunlight—everything went blank. They continued
to sing, lifting me, but nothingness cut across
the screen, and they sang to the dark side,
the hidden one, asking God to help me, calling his name
while a machine breathed for me, pumping,
the essential in and out, lungs balloon,
then collapse: *inspire, expire.*

I've heard that anesthesia is a state close to death,
that the body can mistake this enforced closure, this
shutting down—the bones of the cranium
still their soft swelling movement,
the cerebrospinal fluid ceases its flux, its tides calmed: what
can the body know of this? the brain has been told: *anesthesia*
(the lying voice, the voice I love) the magic word, word
like chant, like the voice of God pulled from the heavens,
the high note dragged through my limbs (*I'm calling
calling you*) while they sliced through skin, fascia: how
does the body reconcile, the brain now asleep, *consciousness*
under a spell, the dreaming one, dying
for the kiss that will shudder her awake, back
to this life, all its sweet sounds.

At Mohonk Mountain: From a Daughter Not Yet Born

He must have held the camera out at arm's length
to snap the picture, so fully do their faces
fill the frame and so soft the light,
an overcast twilight blurring behind them, lighting
one of her cheeks and the downy hairs
along the side of her neck. My father's head is tilted,
leaning on hers, and he's half smiling.
His eyes are tired, his beard a day old
but still he's handsome, though his dimple shows
as a minor indentation, and his sandy cascade of hair is out of frame.
They must be up high, the line of fuzzy trees cresting
her shoulder and coming by her earlobe
where her crystal earring hangs, caught with light.
They are young here and she is pensive,
staring into and beyond the camera,
the fogged landscape fading up out of the trees behind them
into a silver sky, and a panel of light
falls across my mother's right shoulder,
the collar of her seagreen sweatshirt bleached to white.
She looks so young.
Her face is in shadow, dark as her short hair, swept up and back,
her dark eyes, dark eyebrows, the tilt of her head:
this is the self I could never reach,
or else some part of her self, some necessary
organ like a kidney, or a ventricle hushed and pulsing—
did she mean to keep it from me, or just
didn't know how to share it, or didn't know
I was asking, my fumbled requests couched in other words?
And was it shared with him, or wholly private,
exposed in an instant for the camera,
the deep and nurtured sadness passing over her for a moment,

and he, with his instinct for her, pressing the shutter then.
The smooth plane of her cheek, the cavern of brown around her eye
recall how I would stumble awake as a child
and flip on the light, the sudden glare
exposing her, freezing her
and she'd look up, stunned, gazing at me
from some far, far distance.

Mariposa Grove

Here, giant sequoias, one-thousand-year
dialogue with pines and wind, a few
sparse limbs near the top, parallel to earth,
sentries for the small black and yellow birds
that chat through the branches, back and forth.
Here, another one, and here, another,
endless column urging upward,
as if pull from sky meets push from earth,
the opposing forces fixing each tree
in place. The incense cedars bear
a handful of snow on each outstretched arc
of needles, green and white against the sequoias'
burnt sienna, each tree a hundred feet across,
its shallow network for sustenance, six feet
under the earth, feeding water and sap
through the outer rings, just under the deeply scored bark.
Silence and fullness: light passes
to dark, sun to stars, earth turns around sun:
and stars turn in their cold ether,
and then flare out, one by one.

The Operating Room

Those birds wheeled down to feed on the opened belly: they wanted it.
Each crouches at the ceiling or hangs upside down, a slick steel arm,
lens becoming beak, peering sideways, head cocked. Flesh
peeled back, abdomen open, they breathe into it, they strut,
claws scramble on the thin metal table, they hunker sideways, sink
head into shoulders, they peer: the slow
cutting away of unwanted flesh run amok: *restoration*: making
bloody to restore: isn't this the way of the world?
Here, in this room, is *healing*, slicing
the flesh so it rushes back to itself, smooth and clear, made new,
lifted up, the body's urge for wholeness, to close, to cover,
to hold. Not this stapled skin, not
this blood, but the knit and meld, and the black lumbering
birds, outstretched wings beating air, bearing them away.

Fledgling

A hymn to the lost child, the one
who never-was or almost-was, tiny blastocyst
dividing, furious in its attachments, its industry,
until it let go. When does the soul
enter the body? And when does it let go?
Embryo, small dreamer, what did you know?

*

The body houses the red bird, soft tissue
descending, soft blood wrapped in the muscle. It needs
a soft song, the wind moving in the poplars, the olive branches
shushing at night. It needs a quiet song, the blood sweeping
through its channels. The body holds a red bird, its
wings dust the sides; it flies inside the body's casing,
brushing red color along the side.

*

A high sound in the ear. A song
to the one who never-will, who
sings in my ear, the measure of my own breath
against the chambers of my lungs, the tunnels
of my ear. It sounds like my own breath, like birdsong:
chant of the child who *won't be, won't be,*
won't be, no, never-can-be.

*

Two cents, four cents, pocket full of rye,
who says, she says, nonesuch, why?

*

Not one child. Never beating. Never
under the ribcage. The body holds a yellow bird, no,
a blue bird, *no, not the bird*. It holds the cage, the one
that sings with breath. Air—
the sigh of air, playing through the slats.

O Beautiful Boy

He's crawling up out of the fire. He's coming out
of the white. O beautiful boy,

eyes upturned. His left shoulder mottled, the stone melted, he offers
the stump of his arm socket forward. Head turned up, he's crawling

up to standing. Left knee melted, the stone run together like batter,
long dollop where the leg should be, Vesuvial, cratered thigh. And belly,

ilial crest, abdominal cleft all scarred: mottled gray;
mottled mauve; flesh. But look

how he turns to perfection, how the offered deformity
gives way to beauty, smooth stone, perfect as alabaster. Rising up

from the fire. Rising up to standing. Right knee bent. Head upturned.
As if struggling up from being knocked down. Head craned

up, beseeching.
Those perfect lips. Chiselled cup of ear. Right arm hanging straight

down, the hand having just pushed off
from earth. But the smooth

forearm, the white marble's slow curve through the inner
elbow. The forearm braceleted, a scar circling the young flesh

just below the inner hinge of the joint. And the bruising, radiating out
from the break, the circle where hand and forearm

have been joined again to forearm. As if he's offering the broken arm,
arm hanging down.

As if he can't use it, only the crouched right leg
backing him up. Ruin on one side, and here, in the smooth

marble and perfect curves and beauty, a broken thing: bird
limping and trying to fly, bird whose wing is cracked. The wing

hanging down, circled by the bracelet of its break. The white stone
seeping red around the circle, as if the blood

had been called, the blood had been called
and had risen slowly to the surface.

The Cape

The weather-beaten fence winds up
over the rise of sand, the dune grass matted in waves,
dark at the base, bleached on top. The sky

is low, the perfect gray that reverses
to negative space, so the clouds disappear,
become nothing but space hovering

above the pathway between grass and fence
that climbs the rise and drops again
into nothing. The fence is another gray,

edged in ambient light that traces
the spines' edge and throws the slatted shadow
across the sand. This is the same sky

as in the dream of the house, dark, darker in the dream,
the dome a night sky, close to dawn, the house on the dune,
a window open and curtains blowing out, as if the wind

were sucking them from the house. This house waited
for me, a small Cape, the pitched roof
pushing down, alone on the dune, silvered

in dark gray, a pewter light that cast the sand,
the house, the sky in the same ghosted trace. But the curtains,
white, billowed out the window, and the house

was empty, no soft sounds regular in sleep, no warm bodies
nested against each other, or sprawled open, a child's
small frame embracing the night air. There is no child,

paddling through dreams, turning in sleep,
mouth open, arm thrown back. Only
polished wooden floors, blank walls, rooms unfilled.

The house is empty and it has waited for me,
the curtains blowing in and out, as if
it were breathing. But it is not breathing.

Three

Fugue

Sometimes I was in the body of the young boy.
Blond. Small. The King and Queen were with us. Cups,
lady slipper cups, our boat, deep red, and the membrane
sliding back, something moving toward me.

*

I saw the young Asian boy in the maroon Toyota. I saw
him push himself back in his seat, arm straight,
hand tightening on the wheel, trying on his future.
I saw the tension in his neck, the angle. I knew
he was going to hit me. I moved away. I saw the window,
its shape cut in the air, slide back: a clear membrane, it slid back
and the form advanced toward me, colorless, dense,
invisible, with volume, edges, a shape drawing steadily
toward me, my future approaching my present. I saw him
shift in his seat: I knew he would hit me. It was raining.
The rain was a choir. I steered my silver car
to another lane but he nosed in behind me.

*

Sometimes I was in the body of the young boy. We were
on the river. We were in the boat of lady slipper cups,
flat red fiberglass pontoons between us. We all faced
forward in our cups, pedalling, below the surface. The King
and the Queen were with us. The other boy was a man, dark,
maybe my brother. The Queen wore red velvet, her bodice tight
in red velvet, her black hair piled high on her head.
Head up, she sat still, facing forward. We moved down the river.

Sometimes
I was in the body of the young boy. Blond. An entourage
of vessels trailed us. The dark boy and I detached.
We pedalled our own cups, we shot through the rapids,
white water churning, and slid against black rocks
that leapt out of receding water. We tried
to knock each other over, vaulting
through the rapids, oars overhead.

*

I saw the red Toyota behind me. It was raining. The rain
was wind in the trees, white water. It was a set
of deep voices, drumming across the vocal chords
of wind and asphalt. It blurred the concrete, the cars
on all sides. I braked. The red Toyota didn't.
The clear membrane slid open, the shape bore down,
it rocked to a halt, it hulked on my chest.

*

Sometimes I was in the body of the young boy.

Voodoo

The sound wound its way through steady rain,
sinuous, slithery, a wail
looping through the shh-shh of water
striking bare branches, flat concrete.
I couldn't fit it anywhere, not teenage boys
acting tough in the street, playing rap music
and smoking cigarettes, speaking in grunts.
And not panic, the voice raised to a cry.
This was something else, more rhythmic,
issuing from some lost act, deep
in undergrowth, twisted vines and damp air,
the plumed calls of birds, violet, indigo.
I went to the window and looked down:
alone on this New York City street, a young Haitian,
white cloth wrapped around his groin,
arms raised, hands in fists,
jumped foot to foot, chanting,
the rain streaming down his muscled body.
Remember: it's November and cold
and he's almost naked out there but
he doesn't care, head tranced back and body open
to rain. He slowly cranes his head around,
never breaking step, mouth wide and grimacing,
until his eyes fasten on me
and some distant, submerged part of him
registers my face, a semaphore
from the dead world: concrete and steel,
alien, ruthless, white.

Behind Anger

Tonight I am alone and the sadness is breaking me
the way thin lines run through porcelain.
We could have this fight forever, you and I.
We have it over and over, using different props or words
but it's the same one and I want to say:
come here now, just come here now,
I need to feel the smooth skin of your face,
but if you were here
I would withhold my arm from you:
anger is like that.
It brings its own momentum and has its own will,
and behind anger we are too unprotected,
like houses that stand abandoned, shutters banging,
and fear mutters on whatever blows through.

Manel and I Collected Snakes

Manel's backyard touched mine at the corners
and I'd cut through the witch neighbor's yard
where once I found baby rabbits in a hole

and I'd vault the fence into his mother's flower garden.
I remember an ordinary boy: tall, olive skin, thin face, brown hair.
But as we sat on the grass in the buzzing heat,

Manel would cradle a bee in his hand: one
silver motion to catch it, then he'd press his cupped fist up
as if lifting air and open his palm, a bright salute

to the sun, tossing the bee back—
it hovered for a moment, stunned, then darted away.
We collected snakes from the small patch of woods

down the hill and lugged them back to install
in our menagerie: aquariums and cages lined the walls
of his parents' narrow garage, now too packed

for their car. We had lizards, small quick ones,
whose throats puffed when they breathed, and
lime green chameleons, frogs, shiny garter snakes coiled

and ready. We held them a few days, turned them back,
caught them again a few weeks later. In the small
wilderness, he'd show me how to hold a snake

behind its head, how not to grab the chameleon's tail
or we'd lie on our bellies on the stream bank,
drawn by the water's rush and purl,

watching it for hours, the way the man and woman
who loved volcanos stared into the crater, the earth's deep pit.
Once they saw it, they had to keep going back:

the lava flow a river of light and heat, geysers
of liquid fire spewing from the earth's core.
They made offerings to the Fire Goddess Pele, threw her

orchids and bottles of gin, then slipped closer and closer
to fountains of liquid rock, as the ground
gave beneath their feet, and the earth turned itself

inside out. They gazed in, blasted by the heat
searing the open crater, they hovered over the mouth, they
saw the center, its white heat a wind against their faces

until it killed them.

Worry Beads

On the table the mottled glass beads scatter
on their tiny gold chain loop, tear-shaped,

the last bead a flat glass disk, blue and translucent,
different from the rest, with its swirl of yellow,

its black spot, slightly off to one side—the protector
against all evil, against someone's palm

raised against me, against the Devil,
hovering next to my heart. Quiet, innocuous

on the table, the beads spring into action
when raised by a practiced hand—

like my grandmother's hand when she pinned the evil eye
to my bra—and I practiced until I could make the clicking rhythm,

the beads swinging over two fingers, caught with a third,
looping through the hand, a precise series of clicks

the whole body could walk or sway to.
At the *cafenío*, my grandfather dropped his beads slowly,

one by one, a slower rhythm, consonant with thought.
Of course, he thought in Greek.

He came home to throw his money on the bed,
and at dinner, there was wine to make us strong,

feta and olives, and afterward, demitasse cups
of thick, sweet coffee, and a game of bridge,

the room filling with smoke, the chinking
of coins, my parents' and grandparents' voices rising

abruptly to shouts, the regular slap slap
of cards in the air. I crept around the table

to finger the beads lying by each drink:
my grandmother's deep purple and red, inlaid with rubies,

the others more plain, everyday, like my own amber set,
mostly unused now, a talisman to the time

when I believed a small glass bead could protect me,
this gift from my grandmother: *koubouloi*: ordinary beads

in the aura of her perfume—exotic, travelled—bringing with them
the musk of olive groves at sunset, holy water, jewels.

Lit Windows

We lived in the backyard, by the railroad tracks,
over the dunes from the beach, John in the old tack room,
someone in the stable, someone in the dollhouse. We'd gathered
here; young, we'd drifted in. Each day we baked bread,

the good yeast rising, *onion dill*, *whole wheat*,
and cooked for hours, a whole meal spread
to feed anyone at the table. At night, we'd collect
around a lit bowl, passing its dream of warmth

around the circle, hand to hand.

*

It catches in her throat, this rising, it catches
and her stomach turns over. She's out here, she's

walking down a road at night, she's looking
in all the lit windows, columns of amber

spilling to the yard, a family at the table.
Sixteen on the street, in the fog, she's

walking back to her dollhouse, to a plywood structure
in someone's backyard, where she wakes to earwigs marching

across the plywood's striations so close to her face.
She's wearing hand-me-down, the old dress drags

at her calves, she's shivering along the road—
less than rises in her throat.

*

Each morning, we'd drive to the squid packing plant
where all day, cans rattled on the conveyor
a few feet from our faces and heaps of freshly dead squid
rolled toward us. We stood on wooden flats

over steaming, inky black water, and packed and packed
the cans, the squid huddled together in each can, tails
down, tentacles out. John sat on top and all day
pulled the lever: forward: the fish rolled in;

back: they stopped. He'd watch the rubber gloves—
red, yellow, blue—flashing back and forth
as the fishwives grabbed cans, scooped the squid

down the slanted aluminum tray toward them, and filled
each can, each can packed neatly with black eyes,
multiple beads, a ring of eyes staring out.

*

She's lost, she hitchhiked out here, across
all those miles, in this blue car, that

white truck. Outside Denver, she rested
in the middle of the road at dawn, watching

chrome light strike the Rockies, the ripped tops
of the peaks. She ate feed corn

that bounced from trucks, and helped clear trees
near the desert, brittle tips scraping her legs, sweat

coating her stomach, riding down her sides.
And now she's here, and doesn't know why,

but it's as good as the next, falling
through one day after another, walking the canyon,

oranges and walnuts in her pockets, trailing
one hand along the earth's exposed flank.

*

In the dream, she's running between two cars,
and she's handing the baby to her sister, her family

in the black car, her sister in the back. But the white
car is only inches away, the hubcaps spinning by her ankles,

and she knows either car could drift in and crush her.
Behind her, in the distance, more cars gaining—

she cannot stop. She's helping her sister get settled, she
needs the baby to be safe, and then she looks

around her: flat land, the earth like dust,
a few scrub bushes fanned against the coal

of sun hanging above a dry horizon. Her feet slap down
next to the cars' wheels and as they round the curve,

she pushes off from the fender
and pounds into desert, the dust stirring as she passes.

*

What else does she have in her pockets?
Her bare hands, her own hands, drifting
in the small velvet caves.

Her friends will find her soon, drive up the canyon road
in an old blue pickup truck, calling out to her, riding
the running boards, opening the door to the world

once again. But will she go? Her body will, her body
wills itself over that threshold. But a faint outline of her
stands rooted, hands thrust down, hands

stirring, not even lifting to signal, not greeting
or bidding farewell, not even a paper cutout,
hand hoisted and frozen, waving.

Angels Who Lie Down Upon Us

You have decided to die. And I
can't cleave meat from bone, the heart's
small affections, its racketing hammers.
I am talking to the dead: flock around me,
speak in those whispers I understand.
The trellis twines with wisteria, perfect
flickers of confetti, purple flowers,
small chips, and the corded muscle, stalk
and vine, grips brick, forces it down,
sweet scent driven to weight the air.

You grope the unformed clay of language,
signals confused, and will yourself
over the gaps, as if to hold the connectors, as if
by holding them closed long enough, you could
form the word, but what forces out,
contorting muscles and skewing your jaw,
slurs, distorts—you mean to say *yes, yes,*
but instead, *no,* attenuated, deep
in your throat, wrenches out and I watch it
warp back through the tunnels of your brain,
and your face, how it twists,
soft clay someone has slid a thumb along,
smudged with effort, with shame.

And where are the angels who lie down among us?
Why are they not singing?   **63**

Appeal

At seventeen, Benjy could glide across a swamp, missing
the sucking bogs, each shapely leg and round-toed
boot placed surely on ground that held. We knew
the day I arrived, miniskirt and long hair, at the high school.
He taught me to drive his bucket-seated Sunbeam,
up and down that flat road, Canada geese blanketing the fields.
Never make the car work, hand over mine.

*

When I pulled in, he was leaning against the blue Chevy,
arm above the driver's window, back slightly arched,
one black boot forward, his whole body curved
toward the blond girl in the driver's seat.

He was laughing, his body saying *yes*, offering itself up
to her—I knew that language, the hiss of syllables
up his spine, how the muscles rolled under the skin
of his forearm as he flexed his hand. Each time

he laughed, or shifted his weight, sending energy
down his legs, the membrane—
the heat and light between us—

ripped. It ripped. He was ripping it. Then he moved
through the murky night toward me, as if
each step could stitch his way back.

*

Arrogant, he couldn't hide it. He wore it like a scent
and the judge smelled it, couldn't abide this young man

who stood politely before him, the elaborate politeness a scrim,
this young man with his own sense of order, and sex

coming off him in waves. Only sixteen, he had sold drugs.
So. Drawn back, all through that long last night,

both of us sick with grief, the fear wrapping him like a coat
he'd wear through his days and nights in prison, where he'd turn

pale, his arrogance a thin scrim over his trembling,
over the twilight opening inside him.

*

In prison, he was a waif, days and nights
in solitary, rough blue shirt and pants,
government issue, standard fare.
His skin blanched whiter and whiter, he ambled
to the visiting room, head down, and the moments
stretched between us, stones lined one
after another, each breath hard as rock. I watched
the chafed skin at his collar, thought of pulling
up in my mother's yellow car to his mother's
mailbox, fishing out his letters, forbidden, hidden,
and I'd sit on the flat country road to read,
words tumbled out, driven across the page.

*

I wanted to bake bread and offer it,
to rip the loaf over a grave and feed it to anyone

who came. He was gone.
Out on parole, he'd been stopped. Set up,

friends said, so he slipped out of town, underground.
We hadn't spoken in months. But I could feel him moving,

the pulses at my wrists snapped, mapping his path,
bearing weight and ache, the unsaid words, and time,

time piled up, each day a chunk of mortar
added to the mound. And now, syllables of stone lie

between us, stretching into the distance, one after
another, down the mute hallway of all these years.

For Paul

I have an image of you, Paul: you are
turning toward me, laughing.
Then it goes dark.
This must be in the kitchen of your house
in Florida, the light on your skin bronze,
though I remember that overhead bulb
as unadorned. You are filling
from within with joyousness and it's
spilling from your face as you turn, the boy
in you leaping to touch something up high.
But then the image goes black,
as if the shutter closed and I am left
holding this dark emptiness.
I have not *come to terms*. I cannot
place you away from this world. When I think of you
with tubes down your throat, in the hospital,
unable to talk, I want
to paste over it a picture of you smiling,
and I know it's wrong.
Mourning is for those who are left:
a way to cradle loss and curl around it,
to croon a song that keeps you alive,
but meant, finally, to let you go.
One morning after you'd died, I stayed in bed
to dream: I tumbled through one dream after another
(my tooth hinged from the side; flames
sprouting from each outlet: fire
in the walls of the house) and I woke
with a measure of peace, able to hold your image
a moment longer before it blanked.
For three years you woke each day
with your death leaning against you,
and told no one. Did it wear on you,

the wheel against stone, until
you were polished to a high sheen, until,
when you entered the hospital, you wanted only
to be lifted from the wheel?

Elegy in Wartime

How strange that you appear, three years dead, whole
and somehow, free, on the night we began
dropping bombs on a country in the Middle East. You were clear,
and I let you in, not
an abstract notion of your brilliance
but you, separate from me, and standing there. In the dark,
I was soothed, seeing you again, restored.
                                        On the first day of war,
two men stood in the alley behind my house,
flipping a ten-inch hunting knife
into a garage door—held by the tip, snap of wrist,
the knife rushed to the wood—the thud and whack
of contact, over and over, into the air around us. Each time
the knife stuck, wood shrapnel splintered
and flew until the door was as nicked and gouged
as the plastic handle of the knife the Gypsy boy
offered in return for my husband's bone-handled
knife in its leather sheath. This was Corfu
and we coasted downhill on a small motorcycle,
the wind warm in scrub and olive trees. In the belly
of the curve sat a tent, an open fire, a young pregnant girl
on a blanket. Children circled us, clad in layers
of rags, a little girl, green studs in her ears, dirty pink flowers on
    a gray field,
a ripped cotton dress, layers of color showing in the rents,
and her brother, who motioned
us to stay and ran back from the tent, stopping
to hold out his knife in ritual precision, the knife
hushed and flat on his outstretched palms, his eyes steady,
fixed on my husband's eyes.
                                        Yesterday, in the alley,
two men in a standoff, their own testing ritual

skidding on the edge of violence. One was
dressed in black, his hands rough, his eyes unclear.
The other, blond, kept taking the bet, steadily
losing, until the handle snapped from the knife. They
continued to throw the naked blade, hardly able
to grip the small metal flange where the handle had been,
now just a sharp protrusion, and the blade
orphaned, wild, more fit to hit its mark.

The *Metéora*

The Metéora Monasteries of Thessaly stand on the summits
and in the caves of enormous rocks in northern Greece.

1. Monastery of the Transfiguration: *Katholikón*

In the narthex, two skulls under glass, covered
with wrought silver caps, each cap with a hinged flap
open on top. What shows through is the terrain
of sutures, jagged lines smoothed over, the crown offered
to God. The open cap gives proof:
the skulls of *Athanasíos, Iosaph*: two Orthodox monks,
building stone by stone, the Great Metéoro,
up in the air, no steps, just sheer
rock face, hovering a thousand feet up, a rope and net
lowered to haul supplies: lumber, monks, tools, a few
loaves of bread. Now sheathed
in a glass sarcophagus, the glass smudged
from lips held fervently against it:
oh, invisible shield against lips pressing bone.

The old monk stands in the niche
of a prayer bench and sings. His white beard
covers his chest. He sings. Frescoes pattern
the walls, the vaulted dome. The monk stands
inside the prayer bench, frescoes arching overhead, cobalt
blue, charred gold, visions of each saint
skinned or boiled alive set against
the deep blue that calms the heart. The monk
casts a net of song, almost under his breath. He makes
a circle with it. And stands in it. The walls
charred in places from fire, the air smoky with frankincense,

71

the figures flattened in the Byzantine way:
all perspective flush against the plane of surface,
edges of the figures traced and darkened, two-dimensional
bodies rendered in gold, haloes shimmering;
no, not idols, but emblems:
the saints, Jesus' wracked body lifted from the Cross,
the plaster of the frescoes damp, almost fresh.

2. Monastery of the Transfiguration: Ossuary

Skulls. In a row. In many rows, one
stacked over the next, shelves of skulls. They
don't grin, but are composed, quiet on their shelves,
racked one after the next: those who gave their lives
to God. To the right, their leg bones: a neat pile,
fibulae and tibias sorted by kind, trocanters, those
knobby joints pointed out, one slightly gray, another
stained black. And the skulls: so quiet and still and disinterested.

They are clean, clean: mandible, maxilla,
zygomatic arch, a little graying of the optic socket,
a spread of ochre on the frontal bone, across the sphenoid's
flare. And sutures: bones knit together,
parietal and temporal, hinged to the mandible,
and the now empty scoop, buried deep in the occiput,
for the rotating atlas, the pivot bone for turning
the head, something once caught from the corner
of the eye: slow wonder
of the red bird's wing against the sky.

3. Holy Trinity Monastery: *Agios Triada*

The one-eyed monk sits at the summit,
swoop of rock down to a narrow valley
and a thousand feet back up the facing hill,
where a few tourists stand, gazing across
the chasm. Most turn away. Dusty ravine,
pillows of dust, and scrub oak, live oak, gnarled
twists of bark. Steps carved
in the rock face up to the monastery, thin
slashes scored in stone, penance for those who
would ascend here. But the monk blesses the man
and woman when they arrive, and offers them
pomegranates, the dusty rooms
of artifacts from the 16th century. Three iron bells, riven
to the rock with metal rods, on the highest stone, the valley
a sweep beyond the boulder's soft curve: chiming
and clucking of goat bells carried up the warm wind.
And the small, one room church, smoky, charred
black from incense. Only two monks now, habits
black and stiff, beards fanned against their chests.

In the "museum," moving through the glass cases, peering in
at hammers and scythes now rusted and serene, once
hefted to carve the monastery from rock, she is swept
by longing: home, she wants shelter. Hunger combs through
     her body,
across her covered shoulders and knees, like the wind
brushing rock faces, rising through the valley: *apothémysa*:
     yearning:
shouldering against the calm bells, the cool plaster frescoes,
     the angels
kneeling and clapping against a world of blue.

4. Caves: *Agios Georgios*

Have the hermits' bones been brought down
from the caves? Caves scratched in the side of rock,
gashes in the rock face, flush against the sheer side,
and sticks splayed against the rock face
to make a ladder. Who could climb it? Those ones
who were lost in God, who wanted to climb
from the ladder of their flesh, to sing God's song
to the stones, rocking on the marrow of the body.

They were the first ones here,
one thousand years ago, anchorites
who migrated to perch in the caves. On Holy Days
they descended, black birds gliding down
from heaven, to kneel at *Doubiano*, and sing
the Liturgy, moving through the offices. They took
Communion, the wine biting their dry throats,
they spread the veil of their prayer:

to climb the ladder of the flesh,
to sing God's song to the stones,
to rock on the marrow of the body.

Prayer

In the teeth. The well. The throat.
Bringing her to her knees. This is the crying out:
the knees bending, the slow descent, stretching
cloth along the thigh, shards of glass to receive it,
that fragile kneecap, small cup of bone.
It will touch down and the other will follow.
It will clasp earth and rest its weary head.

*

The prairie extends, mired and snowpatched,
black mud oozing up through low humps of snow.
Cattails pierce upward, now only sticks in clusters,
the white birch range against the darker forest, spindly gestures,
quick marks on a dark page. In summer,
they are supplicants, leaning to and fro, their light-struck
hair thrown forward, and the cattails sing,
each brown moment tufting to white as they cast out their seeds.
But now the river is seized in ice, furrows of water blown up
and frozen and the soft pink boulders lean against
themselves as they pile into wall, and then, seat.
But how can we know which angels will listen?

*

The woman's voice rises in song. Minor-keyed,
her voice climbs its register and stays there, sustained,
its timbre clear, no impulse to resolve. This voice walks
the Thracian Plain, it scales the dissonant hillock,
and rolls down the side of anguish. The *claríno* accompanies her,
its bagpipe whine winding around her, as they crest

the next rise, the *bouzouki*'s strings long grasses in wind.
Her voice, unceasing in its keen, ventures on alone, an instrument
no instrument can follow. There is no closure. It is
the sound of pure grief. Held up, the note elongates,
pulling her through the grain and then, at once,
cuts off into silence.

*

The knee, bent, signals release, signals the giving
in. The woman with the shawl cast
over her head walks through the village on her knees,
umbrella scant protection from the rain. She has
already prayed. And been answered. But now
she asks God to watch her. What is she paying for?
Her knees scrape against mud, pebbles imbedding
in her flesh. Each time the knee touches
earth, it knows surrender: *to restore over*: it knows
relieve me of the burden: *yield*, as the bell ringing: *yield*, *yield*.

*

And the angels? Perhaps they are playing.
They twist and turn, heads inclined, tilted toward
one another, as if listening. What do they hear? The wings
arch easily off the backs, lighter than the draped tunics,
yellows and burgundy and blue. Like teenagers, this one
whispers to another, translucent eyes intent on the other's
face, whose auburn curls frame a gaze attentive
to a private vision. What are they saying? They are a jumble,
they hold a secret inside their almost
human bodies, which lift and sigh—
are they borne aloft by the sheer joyousness of flight?—
No, no, they are rising, drawn up by what they hear.

Notes

Roussanou: The first sentence is a paraphrase of a statement by Odysseus Elytis, quoted from a conversation with a mutual acquaintance.

Return to *Loganíko*: A *psalti* is the chanter in the Greek Orthodox Church; the *Taygetos* Mountains are the highest mountains in Greece, the second highest in Europe; *Georgitsi* and *Loganíko* are villages in the *Taygetos*, in Sparta.

Lament: *Moirología*: *Moiroloía* are Greek funeral laments composed and sung by women, now discouraged by the Church. The lament sections are by mother and daughter, Chrysa Kalliakati and Alexandra Pateraki, from Crete, translated by Anna Caraveli-Chaves, in "Bridge Between Worlds: The Greek Women's Lament as Communicative Event," *Journal of American Folklore*.

O Beautiful Boy: After a classical Greek statue, The Young Athlete—retrieved in 1900 from the wreck of Antikytheia, which foundered in the 1st century BC off the island of Antikytheia— now housed at the National Archaeological Museum, Athens, Greece.

The *Metéora*: The ruins of the twenty original *Metéora* Monasteries—the monasteries "in the air"—stand on rock pillars that rise from the Plain of Thessaly, in northern Greece. As early as the 11th century, monks lived in caves and cells; the first monastery was founded in the 14th century. Although many of the churches are in ruins, their frescoes and icon panels are examples of some of the most magnificent Byzantine painting. Five monasteries are still in operation; *Roussanou* is a monastery for women.

photo by Laura Burke

Joy Manesiotis, born in Pittsburgh, Pennsylvania, received a BFA in Sculpture from Virginia Commonwealth University and an MFA in Poetry from the Program for Writers at Warren Wilson College. Her poems have appeared in *The American Poetry Review*, *The Antioch Review*, *The Threepenny Review*, *Colorado Review*, and *The Virginia Quarterly Review*, among other journals. She teaches at the University of Redlands, in California.

New Issues Press Poetry Series